BROKEN
TO BE
BLESSED
DESTINED TO WIN

Judith Gayle

To: Dean
Deeee!   2015

Gospel 4 U Network

Published by

Broken To Be Blessed: Destined To Win

By Judith Gayle

Published By
Gospel 4 U Network

Unless otherwise indicated, all Scripture quotations are taken from the King James Version of the Bible.

Some names in this book have been changed to protect the privacy of the individuals involved.

Editors:
Roschelle Salmon-McKenzie
Stephanie Montgomery

Cover Design
Lerone Moncrieffe, G. Stero Designz Creative Studios

Photo by
Coche Productions, Bronx, New York

Printed in the United States of America
ISBN 978-0-9896249-1-6

CONTENTS

CONTENTS CONTINUED

Acknowledgement

I want to express my profound gratitude to God who has given me the strength to write this book and to declare that through His strength, I can do all things. The journey wasn't easy, but I received encouragement from friends and those who understand what it means to be chastened and restored.

I thank my mom for not aborting me when she was influenced to. Thanks to Pastor Fitzroy Kerr and Pastor Wayne E. Palmer for their continuous prayer and words of encouragement in the midst of the fire which I was going through while writing this book. Thanks for reminding me that God had a plan for me to come out victorious. Natalee Henry, thanks for being on top of everything in my ministry, for making sure I stayed focused and for formatting this book. May God bless and keep you in all your endeavors. Thanks to Joanna Birchett for pushing me to stay focused and get this book out in spite of the devil's attempt to distract me from going forward. Thank you Joanna for staying on top of things so that my voice can be heard through this book.

Thanks to Bishop Michael Frith for his prayers and encouragement. Sir, it meant much to me. Thanks to Brother Wayne Johnson, Sister Cora Williamson and the VOP family for believing in and encouraging me, and never one day doubting my genuine character.

Thanks to Roschelle Salmon-McKenzie and her mom, Ms. Rowena Salmon, for providing a home in New York where I could be comfortable to write this book. I cannot repay you for what you have done, but God will. Dahlia Blake you have been a tower of strength and I will cherish every moment that you have taken out of your busy schedule to encourage me. Thanks to Prophetess Vanessa Anderson, Pastor Delroy Chambers, Bishop Hibbert, Pastor Roger Weller: your words of encouragement, prayer and fasting were towers of strength during the writing process of this book; your support is greatly appreciated.

Thanks to everyone. Those whose names have not been mentioned I appreciate you all. Most of all thanks to my enemies for being my destiny helpers. You have pushed to me to write this book. After all, the word of God is true;

> *What the enemy meant for evil God has used it for good.*
>
> ~Genesis 50:20~

Foreword

During my early formative years, I developed a fondness for the eccentric, the uncommon, or what was considered a novelty to most of my peers. For the most part my exposure and choices in life have helped to crystallize my appreciation for the exquisite and finer things of life. When I first met Judith, it was at a function where I was invited to be the keynote speaker to share from my newly published book, "*Armed and Extremely Dangerous*". Judith sat quietly and unassumingly to the side of the auditorium, and as the night progressed our host invited her to minister in song, and Oh my Lord, when that petite framed young lady took that microphone the place became electrified and charged with the presence of God! That's when I said, "Yes, here is a gem, and one of the chosen vessels of the Lord."

I have always been keenly aware that the most precious things in life were produced under pressure, namely diamonds, gems, pearls, and even oil; and often to appreciate and appropriate their value or worth they had to be mined and refined. The same is said to be true about people who would live with distinction and make their mark on the global scene. There is a popular saying, that, "The anointing makes the difference", and it is so popular now that almost everybody claims to be "anointed", but I can truly say that in Judith's case, it is not merely a saying but she is truly anointed.

In today's Christian circle, there is much to do about whose anointing command an audience, and is heavy enough to shift an atmosphere. Judith Gayle is one of the few names that will always be among them. While a gifted or anointed person may indeed be a rare find, I am always more concerned however, about the story behind the glory. There is a popular song which says, "You don't know the cost of the oil in my alabaster box". As a preacher myself, I am fully aware that in order to carry such a weight of glory, the individual must be pulverized and processed through much pain in order to flow. We may appreciate the olive oil produced by the olive, but the olive is usually beaten and thrashed in order to be appreciated. The beating and thrashing of the story behind Judith's anointing plays itself out in this book.

Broken to be Blessed, Destined to Win is indeed the panorama of Judith's pulverized life that has enabled her to carry such a weighty anointing. This book is engaging and revealing. It dares to break out from the taboo of hush-hush, and strips the veneer of pretense, accomplishments and achievements to give us a heart-moving glimpse of the difficulties that one must overcome to emerge a winner in life.

I believe the frankness and transparency that Judith displays in dealing with her difficult upbringing and social challenges will help to bolster those who feel estranged in their environment and might be struggling with internal woes and external foes. *Broken to be Blessed* is a great biography that reminds us that life is made up of ten percent of what happens to us and ninety percent of what we do with it. Getting better, not bitter is a choice.

We can all take a page or two from this book to help us get from life's setback to a good comeback. It is enlightening and gives a greater appreciation for the oil in Judith's alabaster box. Thank you Judith for trusting us with your life, and for your uncommon transparency, you can now join the apostle Paul in saying, *"From henceforth let no man trouble me: for I bear in my body the marks of the Lord Jesus"* (Galatians 6:17). You are a gift to the body of Christ, thank you for your contribution.

Dr. Michael A. Frith, Ph.D

Introduction

There has been a war for the soul of man from the day Adam and Eve sinned in the Garden of Eden. The war became more intensified when Jesus was born and was crucified. None of us know the path our life will take; we could never determine that; neither could our parents. In this book my life's journey can be describe as a nation catapulted by a tsunami. It might be shameful to say, but I was born out of wedlock, raped, and married to a man who was in the occult (not knowing he was), which lasted a month and a half.

Did I choose my life? No, I did not! Bad things happen to good people; but through the shed blood of Jesus Christ, coupled with wisdom, knowledge and understanding I can live my life the way God intended it to be.

From the day I was born the enemy knew I would have been a threat to his kingdom. So he used all these unseemly things to try and derail my path.

During the process of writing this book, all hell broke loose in my life again. I sat and watched my name being dragged through scandal, shame, disgrace, slander, and deception, but God said, *"write this book."* He assured me of Deuteronomy 33: 27 - *The eternal God is thy refuge, and underneath are the everlasting arms: and he shall thrust out the enemy from before thee; and shall say, Destroy them.* God was carrying me and with His everlasting arms, He was upholding me. I had to obey even though many times I wanted to quit writing this book. Nonetheless, I can tell you that through the eyes of Jesus Christ I was, "Broken to be Blessed –Destined to Win."

Chapter One
The Beginning

I was born in one of the fourteen Parishes in Jamaica -namely Clarendon, in a small town called Chateau. Today, it's a place that is known for gangs and *"don-men"*, but in spite of all that, God chose for me to be born there.

My family background is not one that people would consider ideal. Our small town consisted of mostly poor, domestic laborers. My mother did not have any professional skills; she was a household helper for a local millionaire. Although he was married and had children, he was not satisfied. He enticed my mother with the promise of monetary gain in exchange for sexual pleasure. As a naïve and poor country girl, she was easily persuaded. She was seeking an escape from poverty and with her self-esteem in tatters, she was easy prey. She became his victim - never reaping the promised rewards.

My mother may not have received wealth and riches, but she did gain something from this adulterous relationship -me. When she found out she was pregnant, her friends encouraged her to have an abortion. After all, how would she live with the shame of having a child out of wedlock with a married man? She was confused, but decided that she would endure the shame and carry me. I believe and will never doubt that God had a plan for me, and she could not have touched what God - in His sovereignty, had ordained to walk this earth. The enemy cannot abort God's plan!

According to the Mosaic Law, women like my mom should have been stoned to death, but the shed blood of Jesus has redeemed us from the curse of this Law. His shed blood is the reason why I was not aborted. It is the reason why I stand here today to declare the works of God and to be a servant, helping to redeem others who might be in the same position. Purpose can never die!

Chapter Two
Hidden

It may seem like having a millionaire for a father would be an ideal situation, however that was not my reality. He was determined to keep secret, that the little country helper was carrying his child. Such news would have been considered a low-down, dirty shame among his circle of friends. He was a well-established business man and restaurateur, who was respected in the community and had a prominent position of influence. To cover his sin, he fired my mother and sent her back to the country. Oh yes, he had power and was not afraid to use it.

Can you imagine the shame my mother endured? A young country girl, returning home with dashed dreams - unmarried and pregnant. She was unsure of her fate and did not have a prepared response for her critics. Until the time of my birth, she was an outcast in her community. She told me that she labored with me for two weeks (even though that sounds a bit abnormal).

Although it's not visible, I was born with birth defects - yet in spite of this, I was born for a purpose.

My mom's name is Olive, but I call her Talive because I was unable to pronounce her name (I still smile when I think about that). I love my mom dearly and as I write, tears are flowing down my face because she never had the opportunity to enjoy her life as a young girl. She endured a great deal to bring me into this world by being repeatedly humiliated and suffered shame. My father did not support me, which meant my mom had to struggle through the court system to get maintenance assistance from him. I love and respect her for all she did; most of all, for not aborting me.

There are times when I ask God, *"Why do women have to suffer at the hand of those you've called to be the head of women?"* Sometimes it seems that most men don't know the value of a woman. They often abuse, torture and use women for everything except their God-given purpose. Women, in most cases, are viewed as sex symbols. Yes, I know there are women who give themselves freely to be used in this manner, however I believe even that behavior is born from brokenness. I really wish that women and men could see that God gave us to one another for more than just sex. Women are humans and have rights like everyone else.

Mother, I thank God for you and I will do what I can to make sure you are comfortable in your golden years.

Chapter Three
Growing up

My mom kept moving from city to city, trying to find a place where she believed we would have a stable foundation. As far as I can remember, I never stayed at one school for too long. I think I changed schools about ten times, going from one parish to another. I never got the chance to settle like other children, but my mom was trying her best.

Without having any formal job skills, my mother became a market laborer. She hustled in the market, selling material with a lady named Ms. Ranch. When Ms. Ranch was not looking, my mother would *"borrow"* some material to make dresses for me. I was still her little girl and she wanted me to wear nice clothes. At the time, I didn't understand that what she was doing was wrong and really didn't care anyway. Now, I know it was wrong - but I also understand that she was doing what she thought she needed to.

Occasionally, my father would come to the parish to get goods for his business and pitying my mother, he would give her goods and money. I believe these generous moments only occurred because my mother had a *'grand-aunty'* who was also wealthy and she would use her influence to pressure my father to comply with the court's order.

Like many children growing up in poverty, I never knew what it was like to go to school and learn on a regular basis. I went to school when my mom could send me, sometimes with holes in my shoes and no food to eat. On top of that, I had to walk long distances - rain or shine.

In my early teenage years, my father decided to tell his wife about me. He also allowed me to live with him. Oh, how I thought I would be so happy living with my wealthy father - but in reality, it was more abusive than anything else. Verbally, my father would let me have it. He called me names such as, *"stupid"* and *"nappy-head country girl"*. I couldn't hang out with the kids of his rich friends because I wasn't qualified enough and might embarrass him- especially when I spoke. He bought me the cheapest material for my school uniforms, which were really hard to iron. I had to iron them myself, even though we had a helper.

I went to a Catholic school at the advice of one of his employees. For some reason, Louise was the one worker who I think he feared. She was his best employee and he didn't want to lose her. She baked the best breads, cakes and pastries. Her daughter went to Holy Trinity Secondary, so she told him to send me there as well. He complied with her request, but I never had the opportunity to graduate from that school.

He was cheating on his wife (again) and I was sent to stay with the *"sweetheart"* who lived close to the school. Actually, he used to hide me there before he finally told his wife about me. It was a crazy situation because Ms. Yvonne, (the sweetheart), was cheating also. She would tell my father that we were going to church, but she was really *'churching'* with another man. Instead of going to church, we would head back to her house and I would have to play outside with the other children, while she went inside with her lover.

On a particular Sunday evening when I was thirteen years old, my father arrived at the house. I was so glad to see him. I held on to his hand and jumped up and down with excitement. Of course, he was more interested in seeing Ms. Yvonne. I told him that she was inside with her friend. I followed my dad into the fully-furnished apartment he had rented for Ms. Yvonne (it was a posh apartment).

I was shocked when we walked in because it was the first time I had ever seen a naked adult. My dad wheeled me out quickly and told me to go back to my friends and play. I told my friends what I saw. My dad said he would pick me up later and you could see the shame and embarrassment on his face. He walked away with only a vase of flowers in his hand.

Be not deceived; God is not mocked: whatsoever a man soweth that shall he also reap.

~Galatians 6:7~

Chapter Four
Back To The Country

My father was a player and he had his games well organized. Eventually his wife - whom he abused so badly divorced him and took half of everything with her. He would often tell her that even his dogs were better than her. It was probably a blessing for her to escape that marriage.

After the divorce, he continued his relationship with Ms. Yvonne. She was supposed to be his soul mate. She had a son named Bruce and because my dad loved her, Bruce got the best of everything. He went to a good high school and was well-supported. As a matter of fact, everyone thought that Bruce was my dad's son. At this point, I was able to come out of hiding and live with my father.

Just like his wife, Ms. Yvonne decided to leave too, but it wasn't long before another business woman was on the scene. Ms. Inez had three children and I did not like her at all. Since my mother wasn't around, she treated me in the worst way. One day she took me shopping; I was so happy, but it was soon crushed. After returning from the shopping trip, Ms. Inez fabricated a story and twisted what I had said concerning my father. She also went into my school bag and found a letter I wrote to my mother, expressing my regret about living with my father, instead of her. Although my mother was poor, I would rather have stayed with her.

After hearing her lies, my father chose to believe Ms. Inez over me. What kind of father would put another woman over his own child? Sometimes I think he was just a sperm donor and that my mother would have been better off going to the sperm bank. He surely couldn't deny me, but at the same time, he did not affirm me as a father should. He rushed to pack my things and soon I was back in the country. It was as if they were waiting for the perfect opportunity to get rid of me.

Mothers are precious in the sight of God. My mom was happy to have me home with her and I was more than happy to be home. It was a difficult journey for my mother however. In addition to having her fourteen year-old daughter back home, she had two other children by a man who wasn't much different from my father.

If you ask my mother, she will tell you that I was the one child she could always count on. I wanted to make her proud in every way, but it was not an easy time for us. My mother raised us the only way she knew how. She told us some harsh words and suffered abuse as a result of her constant state of frustration. It was extremely difficult raising three children without the help of a father.

I have never seen my mother with a male in the one-room house where we lived for most of our lives. Yes, I have sisters and brothers by her, but I've never seen her with a man. Whenever we discovered her pregnancy, it would hurt me because I knew she didn't have the financial resources to support her children. Sometimes we just had hot water and salt for tea, or used salt as toothpaste. Our bed consisted of old clothes on a spring that was used as a mattress. Only God knows how we survived, or why she allowed the abuse to continue.

After my father returned me to the country, I started going to a nearby church. I would come alive at church, participating in Sunday school and other activities. I was a master at Bible Quiz - you could not beat me at that! As the years went by I realized I could sing, which was a great discovery for me. The pastor would always take me with him to sing and I was everyone's favorite in the church. There was not a concert or rally that our church attended, where the *"singer girl"* (as I was affectionately called), would not perform. I was the little start of the church. I sang the same song every time - "Now the Circle Won't Be Broken".

There was a particular, notable family at the church. They had a son named Gary, who liked me. One day, my father asked me to come to Kingston to get money. Gary was also going to visit his sisters in Kingston, so we decided to go together. Of course we didn't tell anyone except my best friend, that we were taking the same bus. I never imagined that she would tell the entire church.

When we came back from Kingston and returned to church, I had an unforgettable experience. It was one of those services where everyone was in the spirit. People were surrounding me and speaking in tongues. I can still remember some of the "tongue language"; *"my-my-can-do"* was the most famous.

After the service, one of the ministers called me into his office and asked me if I had committed fornication. Although I heard the preacher mention fornication many times, I didn't know what it was - but since Gary had kissed me good night, I said yes. The following day they called my mother and told her to prepare me for baptism. I didn't understand what was going on, but I just went with the flow because I really thought I did something wrong. Gary got baptized too and never spoke to me again.

Shortly after that incident, I began attending another church. I sang often at the new church and really felt like a part of the pastor's family. I spent a lot of time at his house because his children were musicians, so it was a joy for me to be there. It was not normal for me to have quality, family time so I soaked up every moment. My mother was happy to know that I was with people of substance.

The Coburn family started a group called The Crusaders. We were the talk of the town and other groups were intimidated when we were on the scene. When it came to ministry, we were unstoppable. I was proud to be a part of this group - especially as a lead singer. Eventually, the group disbanded and everyone went their separate ways to pursue their own dreams. To this day, people still ask me about The Crusaders. My response is usually the same - *"nothing lasts forever, except salvation"*.

Chapter Five
Discovery

After visiting my father, I discovered that I had a brother who was living in Negril, which is one of Jamaica's top tourist destinations. He owned cottages and a sports bar, and was involved with water-sports equipment as well. I was offered the opportunity to visit him, which was the beginning of a new life for me. I sat on the beach and watched the tourists as they passed by or listened to the beach musicians sing Harry Belafonte's songs. I loved it so much that I started signing the songs as well. It was a joy to experience so many new things.

While I ran my brother's business, there were two other young ladies - Hopia and Charm who took care of their dad's business as well. Negril was the party capital of Jamaica, so in our free time we always hung out at one of the clubs called Compulsion. We were living the party life; there was not even time for sleep. You could do whatever you wanted and no one was there to stop you.

One day we went clubbing and a guy came over to ask me for a dance. My friend Hopia said, *"Leave her alone. She's a Christian."* When I think about this story I laugh. Did she just say I was a Christian? If so, what on God's green earth was I doing in a club? That's what happens when you lack true spiritual guidance - you do things that are wrong, but think it's ok to do them. I was exposed to another side of life and for me, it was not as boring as living the Christian life. I was among people with money and there were no limits placed on when I could go out or come in. I had a boyfriend with whom I became intimately involved. Oh, what a change!

One day while singing at my brother's boat bar, I was approached by a gentleman who thought I sang like Whitney Houston. He asked me if I would sing at a hotel. I agreed without reservation and told him I only knew two Whitney Houston songs that I learned in school: The Greatest Love of All and One Moment in Time. I sang those songs at Hedonism II for about a month, until one day a young lady named Nadine came to me and said she was tired of hearing those same songs. How rude was she? She was right though, so I asked her to help me get some new material. Nadine was from a duo called Mello and Jello. They were really popular in Jamaica, but when I met her, the group no longer existed. She was very helpful.

I enjoyed singing in the hotels. I was getting in deep and I loved it. There was something about me that was really different from the other singers. Although I was exposed to the same things they were - there were certain things I could not do. I found myself in the company of homosexuals, drug lords and pimps. Everybody wanted to sleep with everybody, no one cared about morality and truthfully, I could only go but so far. Once, I dated a drug pusher and when he went to jail, I collected the money for him. There are some things I will not disclose, but let's just say it was a really dirty life. When I was collecting money, I was very afraid. What was I doing? This was not how I was raised, but the path where life can lead will either make us or break us. I would never go to bed without praying and asking God to help me see another day.

I became famous in the hotel industry, expanding my reach from one to twelve hotels. Soon, I started opening for their New Year's Eve functions. One time they had Stephanie Mills, The Boys and Diana Ross at Grand Lido Hotel and I had the opportunity of being the opening singer for that night. I was a part of every big event that took place in that area and didn't play when I had a microphone in my hand.

I left the hotel industry in Jamaica for a while and spent eight months in Mexico singing at a club called Mango Tango. This is where I taught Chuck Norris (the movie star) to dance the "dollar wine". After returning to Jamaica, I continued performing in the hotel industry. There was never really a dull moment in the secular music world. It wasn't the perfect scenario - however I will not kill my past, because it drives me to understand my future.

Chapter Six
Family Abuse

Living with my brother on the hotel compound was an intense experience. Everyone said that he was a drug addict, but I wasn't able to see the signs right away. I watched my brother daily, observed his every move and heard everything he did. He would go into the bathroom and pretend to shower seven to eight times a day, but there was no denying the scent that escaped from his window. Of course, he always blamed it on the extreme heat. We lived by the sea-side, so he could have easily gone for a swim. I later realized that the foul odor came from the drugs and it was enough to make you sick.

While sleeping one night, I felt a knife at my neck. It was my brother - on top of me, telling me that if I screamed he would kill me and bury me under the sand. I had to lie still while he forced himself upon me. I was a victim of my own biological brother. Addicts think that they are the smartest people God created and are always making excuses for their behavior. He told me that since I was his half-sister it was okay to sleep with him, and because he threatened my life, I didn't fight him. There was nothing I could do. He sexually violated me on two separate occasions.

I was completely overwhelmed. I couldn't keep this secret any longer, so I told a guy from the band at the hotel. His name was Bobo. He was married, so I trusted that he knew about life. He rescued me from that situation; rented a place for me and taught me how to live on my own.

I never lived with my brother again, but I still had to deal with the trauma of what he did to me. Forgive him? I didn't even know what that was. I knew he could not touch me again, but despite this, it was too late. I was already wounded. I thought that if my brother could do this to me, it must be the norm or expectation for other men to treat me the same way. As a result, I was repeatedly sexually-abused by other men and had mistaken sex for love. Rejection became the order of the day. No one wanted to stay with me; they just wanted to have fun. Each time, I was left with more scars.

If you're reading this book and have ever been sexually-abused by a family member, I understand how you feel. I understand how the shame hangs over you and how the anger wants to take hold of your life. You wonder if anyone will believe you and you cry yourself to sleep. It leaves a scar that is extremely deep - but not deep enough that God cannot heal it.

Chapter Seven

The Transformation

New avenues began opening up for me. I was approached by Gayle Jackson, one of the owners of the Negril Tree House. Gayle knew the owner of Jahboy Productions in Atlanta, Georgia. She introduced me to the owner of the recording company, who was willing to sign me. I was very grateful for the opportunity. They brought part of the studio to Jamaica and I traveled to the hotel every day to record.

After the album was finished, my life took another turn. In 1998, my mother wrote a song for me which I sang at a popular song festival and won second place. I won some money and gave it to her. It was the first time in her life that she had enough to spend on herself. I was proud to be able to do that for her, knowing that it made her happy.

The hotel became my life - I loved it. I discovered a way to make money, which removed the bondage of dependence from my parents and family members. I felt independent because I was my own boss. I had a business in Negril that my mother was running for me, and a chicken farm in the country. I sang background for Dancehall singer, Richie Stevens, and I had a song with Dancehall singer, Lady Saw. I also had a recording contract. What more could I ask for?

If I had listened to my father, I would have been a dressmaker. At that time, they were not called fashion designers and dress-making was considered a low-class job, especially in the eyes of my father. He put down everyone who did this type of work, yet he wanted that for me. Oh, no! I would never be what he declared I should have been. I was determined to succeed and come out to be something good in life. Sometimes I think he was a wicked man who never knew the true meaning of life. He was cold to everyone - except his dogs, Rex and Betsy. He took them to the vet, but he never took me to the doctor.

Although I was making money, I believed in education and had a strategy to learn everything I missed by not finishing school. I only associated with friends who had graduated from high school. When they spoke *"big words"*, I pretended like I knew what they were saying. I would then get my dictionary and look up the meaning. It was then that I realized that a particular word was spelled differently than I thought. After learning the definition, I was then able to use the same word in a conversation with someone. I was so proud of myself. Many of my friends will never know that I did not graduate from high school, unless they read this book.

In the book of Genesis chapter 11, Shem, the son of Noah produced a generation that spoke the same language. They became so powerful that they started building the tower of Babel. God made it clear that they could accomplish any thought that were devised in their minds. When God saw their plan to build a tower to heaven, God had to step down from heaven and confound their language - stopping them from accomplishing their task. I say this so many will understand that whatever the mind can conceive - we as humans can achieve. That was the strategy I developed to learn through others and I was determined to reach my goal and all my aspirations.

By then, I wanted nothing more from my father and he became a distant memory. I would often visit my mom to make sure she was well taken care of, but I had my life to live too. I made my job in the hotel my top priority. One night, I went to one of the hotels and did a performance that was out of this world. At the end of the night, I turned to my background singer, Cheryl, and told her that I always wanted to feel this burst of energy after each performance. I loved the feeling of knowing that I gave everyone something to remember. That was my last night singing in a hotel. I had my own plans, but God always has a better plan.

Chapter Eight
I Surrender

We do not know the path life will take, but we live day to day with the hope and trust that we will be all right. I rarely went to church anymore and if I did, it was to a Catholic church where the priest did his thing while I slept or talked. I loved to party, but there was always a fear in doing everything *"worldly"*. For some reason, there was still that fear of God on my life, even though I had left the church. I was enjoying life as it came, but I took nothing for granted.

By this time, my mother had become a Christian. She would gather with other ladies at prayer meetings and they would bombard heaven for me to return home like the prodigal son (Luke15:11-32). Their wish would soon come through.

It was a beautiful Thursday morning when I woke up to the sun peeping through the windows. As usual, I started my day by thanking God for another day; then strange things started happening to me. I began to cry. I thought to myself, *this does not make any sense.* I had everything for my comfort. There was no lack in my life. I lived in a three bedroom, completely-furnished house all by myself. I could change my car every year if I wanted to. Money was not an issue for me. Guys didn't call me - I called them! Since I had the money, I was in charge of my destiny, especially with men, and no one would dare come to my house without giving me prior notice. I was living large according to the world's standard, yet deep inside I realized I was not happy. Something was missing, but what could that be?

With the tears rolling down my eyes, I heard a voice say, *"Pray."* Just imagine my reaction to that! What in the world was going on? I got up from the bed and stood by the bedside. Believe me when I tell you that I felt something knock me on my knees and I fell to the ground, pleading, *"Help me, God."*

That same weekend, I was planning to see an old boyfriend who was married. Can I say that again? He was married. I can imagine your eyes wide-open right now. He was the nephew of a prominent Jamaican reggae band artist. We met a few years back when he came to Jamaica on vacation. At first, we were just good friends and I respected his marriage. Then he began telling me his relationship wasn't what he expected and that he was no longer in love with his wife. So, we started seeing each other and ultimately became lovers. We had been separated for a while and this weekend was planned for us to reconnect and rekindle the fire.

I began my journey to Kingston early that Friday morning. A few days earlier, I received a call from the pastor's son stating that my old church was having a convention starting that weekend. I thought it would be a good gesture to drop by the church and say hello to my former church family, while I stopped for a visit with my mother. I didn't mess around when it came to church, because I had seen enough miracles to know that God was real and that He was always in control. In spite of this knowledge, I saw Christians as poor and always begging - especially in light of how I was now living. The word of God reminds us that…

the king's heart is in hand of the Lord, as the rivers of water: He turneth it whithersoever he will.

~Proverbs 21:1~

I stopped by for a visit with the pastor's children and we talked about old times at church. Those were good times for us as teenagers. I wanted to leave before the pastor returned, but it was too late. I heard a voice that I did not want to hear - it was the pastor. He was a man of faith and I did not want to see him or hear him chastise me about the path I had taken in life. Growing up, I saw great miracles wrought through him and I did not want to disappoint him. He came upstairs and remarked that he had not seen me in a long time, except for on TV. Then he asked if I was coming to church. I told him that I wouldn't be able to attend because I was on my way to Kingston and was just stopping by for a quick hello. He didn't respond, except to ask me to stay for prayer. There was no way that I would turn down prayer - especially from him because he was very powerful. I remembered once when he was preaching at a church and he made an altar call, requesting three young men to come for prayer. They refused and later drove away. It was not long after their departure that news came back to the church. They were in a terrible accident. Two died and one lived to tell the tale, but he was without legs. For that reason - when I remembered that story - I stayed.

The church was so hot, but there were some fine, good-looking brothers there. What? I was a sinner. I had a license to sin. I was sitting in the front right by the pastor's daughter, so I could see everything and everyone who passed by. I turned to the pastor's daughter and said, *"The brothers are looking good."* She said, *"Judith, behave yourself."* I behaved myself, but that did not change the fact that the brothers looked good.

I don't remember the topic of the sermon, but I could never forget the lady that went up to sing. Her name is Carol Carridice. Her song touched me in such a way that I will never forget: *"I got a roof up above me, and a good place to sleep, food on my table and shoes on my feet, you gave me your love Lord and a fine family, thank you Lord for your blessings on me."* I was moved by those words. As I sat in my seat, I began pondering things that were not ordinary for me. I thought that if she was singing those words, then it would be okay for me to get saved.

The night progressed and the sermon was preached, but the song was still in my head. When it was time for the altar call, I found myself right there. I couldn't resist the part when they asked if anyone wanted to give their life to the Lord. With tears streaming down my eyes, I said yes to God again. I could hear voices telling me that I'd made the wrong decision. How would I survive? The only thing I knew how to do was working in the hotel and that was financing all my other businesses. I thought I had just made the worst move of all.

After the altar call and the congratulations, what was next? I headed for my destination just the same. I was happy to see my boyfriend and was still thinking about the good times that were planned, but my entire system was shut down. He begged me that night for intimacy and I would have loved to give in, because he was good at what he did. So even if we broke up, that alone was enough to draw me back to him, but I'd made my decision - that was the end of it for me. I could never give myself to him again. A change was wrought and God was now in total control.

That Saturday morning I got dressed and went out to buy clothes to wear after my baptism scheduled for that night and for church on Sunday. I called my friend Deveral, from the Coburn family and told him about my transition. He thought I was lying and made a big scene out of it. He told me that I was not serious and would quit in no time, but he and his wife still followed me to shop for the clothing I needed. After heading to the church, he gathered his friends, some colleagues and they all came in the van to see if it was true. Oh, yes it was! I was immersed under the water and came up a brand new creature. The old Judith was no more; she was buried.

Chapter Nine
The Journey

I was now saved, water-baptized and filled with the Holy Spirit. It was the beginning of my new life. I had no clue what was ahead; my head was in spinning mode at this juncture. I had left Westmoreland with very little in my car. How was I going to face all my people? What would they think of me? What would I tell the hotel owners about my contract with them? Where would I live? Since I was an adult, I couldn't look to anyone in my family for help. Just imagine the position I was in.

All I could do was head back to Westmoreland and lock myself in the house for days. My phone was ringing and I couldn't answer, because I didn't know what to say to the people from my job. They wanted my head for walking away like I did. I was tempted many times to go back. Thank God for a church sister named Shawna, who had asked for my cell phone number before leaving church that Monday. I believe that God sent her to me, because every time I was tempted, she would call and tell me to come back to Clarendon (where the church was located). I was four hours away, but I decided to take the journey. It wasn't easy going back and forth. Eventually, I made the decision to settle in Clarendon. That was a great leap of faith for me.

At this point I needed help and didn't really know the folks at church. Most of the faces were new and the people I grew up with were no longer there. I wasn't sure what would happen. It was not easy to return to the life from which I had run away. I didn't understand what it meant to surrender and I was just starting to get the understanding of this thing called faith.

I wasn't able to afford my own home at this point, so I lived with Shawna. She was a real source of strength. She loved God and was serious about her walk with Him. I would go back and forth between Shawna's home and the Plummer's home. After Shawna got married, I lived with the Plummers full time. They were very nice people. Ms. Jackie (the wife) was like a big sister to me. She could tell me anything and I listened;

she was always there for me. She was the type of person that could keep a secret. If you went back to her months later, she wouldn't even remember the full details. She was extremely trustworthy and I never had to worry about her revealing confidential information.

When a house across the street became available for rent, I moved out of the Plummer's home. I was now living by myself and was determined to become stronger in my faith. I would spend days in prayer and fasting, because that was a core principle of the church I attended and I wanted to abide by the rules. I wanted to get deep and learn the heart of Christianity, so I started adjusting myself to what was presented to me. I can definitely say that fasting and prayer works! My eyes began opening up to things I hadn't previously understood. I began to have serious dreams about people and things that would happen. When Ms. Jackie saw the manifestation of the things I would tell her, she began calling me, 'Sister Joseph'. If I told you about a dream I had, you could be assured it would happen.

I started singing again in churches and doing concerts, but it was not like before when I was younger. This was a new season and a different generation. In this season, the anointing was the only thing that would make the difference. My friend Shawna heard me sing approximately a week after my baptism. When she heard me, she wondered why everyone said I could sing. I laugh every time I remember that. It doesn't matter how high our range, or how melodious the voice - it is the anointing that makes the difference. I really thought coming into the church from the hotel job with all the skills and singing experience I gained, would make me highly-revered, but I was wrong about that. I was dry.

I can remember performing in a rally at the church. This would be my first encounter with the Holy Spirit. As I began to sing, the crowd started cheering. I felt good, like I was in charge. I wanted to exercise my range the way I used to at the hotel, but I heard a voice saying, *"Stop now."* With my eyes closed, I ignored the voice and continued singing. When I opened my eyes, the church was empty. The same people who were cheering, were now outside getting on their bus. I learned a serious lesson that day. Upon explaining that to a pastor, he told me to watch the flesh and try to understand the working of the Holy Spirit. I was learning, slowly but surely and I was determined to never be in that position again.

I continued to seek God by spending time in the word, praying and fasting. My discernment was getting sharper. Ms. Jackie understood and helped me. Every dream would pass through her and believe me, I was seeing things. There was so much going on in the church and it was all revealed in my dreams. I could not understand this. The pastors were keeping malice; members were keeping malice with sinners and pastors were hearing gossip and using it for sermons.

I had a friend that left the church due to her marriage. The pastor did not consent to her marrying this young man, so she had to leave the church. She was still my friend, but the pastor did not like that. Once he called judgment against someone, everyone would have to stay clear of that person. I never read that in the Bible, so I kept my friend close. Christians should not keep malice with one another

we should seek for peace and pursue it.

~ Psalms 34:14~

She was a good person; she gave me shelter when I gave my heart to the Lord and always gave me good advice. She taught me hair dressing so that I could help in her salon and make a living.

Convention was here and everyone was in high gear. For four days, I took my regular seat on the front bench, but the Bishop would not let me sing a note. Everyone knew it was because of my friendship with the former church member. I told my friend what happened and she said to me, *"I prophecy this day that if he doesn't make you sing, God is going to rise up someone to ask you."*

One night during the offering, he called me to give a chorus of a song. I did just as he asked and God turned the place upside down. The song I sang was, "God Can". Then it was time for the church choir to sing- and pardon me- but they were embarrassing, and I am not afraid to say that. I humbled myself and went back the following night. When he called for the choir to come sing, the guest pastor from overseas interrupted him. He said, *"Sir, can I ask you to let that young lady who sang last night sing instead?"* God has a way of doing things and in due time, He will exalt you if you just trust Him and remain humble. God moved that night and lit that place up, showing man that he was not in control. The guest pastor prophesied to me four times before I could take my seat. First, he said that every time I sing, idols will burst into flames. Then, he told me all that God would use me to do. I didn't really understand all that he was saying because I was inexperienced with prophecy - but I can tell you that history started recording my life from that day, especially regarding the terror I would face.

Chapter Ten
Confrontation

The anointing which ye have received of him, abideth in

you, and ye need not that any man teach you; but the same

anointing teaches you all things and is truth, and is no lie,

and even as it hath taught you, ye shall abide in him.

~ 1John 2:27~

This scripture is so clear to me; I don't need an explanation when I see people being deceived by manipulating the word of God. I don't claim to know all things, but I thank God for His word and common sense. As I began spending more time in the word and prayer, I was in awe of the way God would talk to me.

One day I was at my friend's salon when I overheard a conversation between two unsaved ladies. They were discussing my youth president. I inquired as to the nature of their conversation. They explained to me that instead of being an example, the youth president was in malice with them. As a result, they didn't have any respect for her. When I went to church that night, I asked the youth president if those two ladies were telling the truth. I was dumbstruck when she confirmed that it was true. *"Does Bishop know that you are in malice with sinners?"* I asked. She assured me that he did. I reminded her that the Bible says we are not to stand in the way of sinners (Psalms 1:1). She was so wroth with me that I couldn't say anything else, so I just walked away.

When I went to church the following Sunday, I knew something wasn't right. I became the sermon for the first half of the service and folks were looking at me because some of them heard what happened. I was so mad! I wanted to tell everyone off, including the Bishop, but I had too much respect for the man of God.

I spent the next few days in prayer and receiving counsel from other members of the church, because I was never known for being disrespectful and I didn't want to start now. God's word teaches us not to harbor bitterness in our hearts, so I decided to call the Bishop and ask for a meeting to discuss what happened. He wanted to meet immediately, but I was still angry, so I did not want to go at that specific time. I wrote a letter to him letting him know that I could not face him in my current mood. He was very upset and accused me of being disrespectful for not attending the first meeting. Two weeks passed before I was comfortable meeting with him. I sat down and asked the question, *"Sir, I just want to know if you were preaching about me?"* He never answered the question, not even at the urging of his wife, who was also in the meeting. Instead, he told me several stories and put a curse on me. He said he knew exactly where I would be going to church and what would happen to me. I looked at him and said, *"There is therefore now no condemnation to them which are in Christ Jesus, who walk not after the flesh, but after the Spirit."*~Romans 8:1~

I assured him that I would not say a thing to anyone. His final words to me were, *"I will not be quiet. I will make sure everyone knows how you were sowing discord in this church."* To this day, he has never clarified whether or not I was the topic of his sermon.

I know there are true men and women of God out there, but I will take the liberty of saying they are hard to find. I can only talk about my experience, but I will not say anything degrading about any leader who God has ordained to preach His word. Let every man examine his own life before judging others. I have forgiven him and continue to pray for him and the countless others, who like me, have been wounded in ministry.

Before this incident occurred, I was scheduled to perform at a gospel concert at the church. A few days before the event I had a dream that as I was singing, the Bishop sent the Deacon to take the microphone from me; I just gave it to him and went away. The next morning I was awakened by the ringing of the phone. To my surprise, it was the same Deacon who took the microphone from me in the dream. He said he had a message for me. I told him that I knew he was calling to tell me that I wouldn't be singing at the concert because I had a dream. I relayed the dream to him and he replied, *"Judith I don't need to tell you anything else, God already told you."* The word of God cannot lie.

~Psalm 25:14 says it well: ~

The secret of the Lord is with them that fear him;

and he will show them his covenant.

We don't need to fear anyone because God always goes before us and make every crooked path straight. I went to the concert and watched the Bishop and youth leader point and laugh at me. After the concert, I left and never returned to that ministry again. I didn't know what was ahead, but I knew God was with me.

Chapter Eleven
A New Journey

I started attending another church to ensure that I wasn't left without spiritual covering. I believe that every believer needs to be a part of a local church, so that they are accountable to someone. If we refuse to do so, we will fail and the end result can be catastrophic.

I had no idea how my future would turn out, but God knew. My faith in God was now firm, so trusting God was all I knew to do. I no longer stayed with my friend and the business I was in was becoming tiring. I was delivering goods to different grocery stores two days a week, from one parish to another. Although Ms. Jackie's son, Horace, was working with me, I was the primary driver. There were days where I would spend four hours driving each way. I was so embarrassed when I would run into one of my former colleagues; they would always look at me with disgust. Just like my brother, some of them thought I was an idiot to choose Christianity over my hotel work. Yes, I was tired and there were times my friends made me feel low, but I was determined to stay with God no matter what.

One evening after doing very well in our business, Horace and I were going home. We were playing our music, singing and worshiping God, when suddenly the vehicle went out of control. The steering wheel locked and I couldn't maneuver it. I held on to the hand rail while the van started going down the hill. I turned to Horace and said, *"This is it."* The van was heading towards a light post. I knew that hitting the light post would cause us to hit a rock and then plunge us into the sea. Since there was nothing I could do, I closed my eyes and gave up. Suddenly, it felt like someone picked the van up and put it back down on the road. When I opened my eyes, I saw that the van had landed on a heap of marlstone, instead of hitting the light post. How was that even possible? Surely a miracle had taken place.

I could barely breathe when I got out of the van - this seemed too good to be true. There was a man traveling behind us. He stopped and asked me one question, *"Are you a Christian?"* I replied, *"Yes."* The gentleman told me that he saw everything that happened and that we should keep living for God. After he left, we got back in our vehicle, still not understanding what happened. After driving for another fifteen minutes, I lost control of the van again. It was frightening to see the vehicle moving like a robot. We knocked out four concrete posts and some trees, but the only damage was to the driver's side mirror. Another driver came up and asked us the same question, *"Are you a Christian?"* I gave the same reply, *"Yes."* That was a day that will never be forgotten. Death confronted us twice, but God had a different plan.

We were three hours away from home, but definitely could not drive the vehicle again. A gentleman offered to take us home. Later, when we returned to get the vehicle, we asked for the man who took us home. The people said they didn't know who we were talking about. We couldn't understand why they didn't know him. It is still a mystery to this day, but I leave it alone because that one is just bigger than us.

I decided to stop doing that business. We immediately got a buyer for the van and put the money in the bank. I was based at home until another idea came; opening a book store.

I rented a building and everything was going well for a while. One day I received some advice and because of the person's position, I humbled myself and took it. Our anointing doesn't stop the devil from going after us. He will use anyone who is available, but just like Joseph said,

"What the devil meant for evil, God turned it for good."

~Genesis 50: 20~

The enemy will use every strategy to pull us down and he will not stop until he has exhausted all options. But God will take care of His people. There are many people who are anointed by God, but used by the devil. I wonder how many pastors will preach about the young prophet and the old prophet in First Kings. I don't understand why it's an unpopular topic among preachers. According to 1 Kings chapter 13, there was a young prophet who was given specific instructions by God. He was on the right path until an old prophet heard about his wisdom. He tricked him into disobeying God's instructions and it cost the young prophet his ministry and his life. This story is very meaningful to me because I have seen that story played out in my own life, however I am grateful that the end results were not the same for me.

Chapter Twelve
Tragedy Strikes

One day this man of God came to me and was impressed by how my business was flourishing. He said that I could do better if I had more variety. Since he was a prominent person, I asked for his help. He said that he would think about it and get back to me. I wasn't in a hurry, so I waited patiently for him to return with his suggestions.

During that time of waiting, I had a dream that I went to his place of business. When I got there, I asked for him and he turned his back to me. Then a lady approached me and said, *"He will not give you the money."* I walked away, saddened by her words. The following day - to prove if what I saw in my dream was true- I went to his place of business. After entering his office and chatting for a while, he told me that he could not lend me the money. I was a bit disappointed, but not extremely hurt because God had already shown me the outcome. I just reminded myself that God was with me, so no weapons that were formed against me could prosper (Isaiah 54:17).

This man wasn't just a potential business associate, he was also a friend. He was someone I knew before I got saved and someone I trusted with everything. He would visit my house and we would laugh, talk and share the details of our lives. When he was going through rough times in his life, I was always there for him. That is something I truly believe in; we must be there for others, because we don't know when our time of trouble will come. After a period of time our friendship became something else and we started to like each other. He spent a lot of time with me, so he knew my heart. He also knew that when I cared for someone, they have my full attention. He still visited my store and one day he said, *"When you put your business over God, it will not work. I won't tell you what to do, but it won't work."* My assumption from his statement was that I should close my business.

After he denied me the cash, I was introduced to someone else from whom I could borrow the money. I got the money, but my business went downhill. As a result of this, I became very depressed so I took his advice to close my business. I did not see where I was putting my business over God, but I trusted his judgment because he was a man of the clergy. Also, since he had promised to marry me, I thought it was wise for me to practice obedience.

I would share my dreams with him because he was supposed to be my soul mate. He once told me that God discounts dreams and even showed me scriptures to prove it. After he quoted Ecclesiastes 5:7(NIV);

Much dreaming and many words are meaningless;
therefore fear God-

I cursed my dreams. I thought he knew best because he was a man of God. I did not know that Job 33:14-15 said

For God speaketh once, yea twice, yet man perceiveth it not.
In a dream, in a vision of the night, when deep sleep falleth
upon men, in slumberings upon the bed.

One day he looked at me and told me I was very innocent. I didn't realize that there were people out there who will take your innocence for weakness and manipulate you. I just wanted to be honest and live according to the Bible. I gave my all and surrendered to him, because I believed in the Scripture which states obey those who have rule over you. We were not sexually-involved, but there were moments of intimacy between us. Honestly, it was not something I enjoyed because the Bible tells us that intimacy should only be between a husband and wife. I went along with it however, because I thought he would eventually be my husband.

One night I had a dream where I was holding a baby in my arms and the child was dying. In the dream I was crying and telling someone that the child had not eaten anything for three days. As I prepared to lay hands on the child, I woke up weak and spiritually drained. I went to church and told one of the praying mothers about the dream. She told me to go on a three-day fast. I went to Ms. Jackie and she told me the same thing.

Immediately, I packed my bag and left for the hills to start my fast. It was a time of replenishing for me, but even at the point of your breakthrough, the enemy will still try to defeat you. On the second day of the fast, a lady at the house told me I could break my fast by drinking some tea and continue into the night. At that moment, I heard a voice out of heaven say to me, *"Do you remember when Saul went to Gilgal to wait for Samuel to make the sacrifice?"* I jumped immediately and shouted, *"NO!"* in such a way that would frighten anyone.

We need to know God for ourselves because
the devil is like a roaring lion, seeking whom he may devour.
~1 Peter 5:8~

The devil will use anyone who is available, whether you wear the biggest robe or the smallest. At the end of the fast, my eyes were seeing things in a greater way than I could have imagined. If you had a million demons, I could see them - it was something amazing to experience.

When I went home I visited Ms. Jackie. She told me that my friend was looking for me, because I did not tell him I was going away. One thing about me is that I love God and will give up everything to please Him. If I find out you are walking contrary to His word, I will talk to you, but if there is no change, I'm gone. When I finally saw him, I said, *"Is there something wrong with kissing someone who is not your husband?"* He said, *"Yes, because it can lead to other things."* I looked him in the eyes and told him that I would not do such things again. I was bold, but I did not care. We talked for a while longer and then he left.

The little gain I had from the store was getting low. Days turned into weeks, weeks turned into months and finally it was finished. I hid this from him for two months by going to Ms. Jackie for breakfast and dinner. Eventually, I called him and asked for his help. He told me he would help me in two weeks. I waited until the two weeks passed, then I called him and asked if he remembered his promise. He said he remembered, but just couldn't help me. I was speechless. He then said, *"In all you do, guard your heart."* I asked what he meant by that, but he just repeated the statement and hung up the phone. After a few minutes, he called back and told me that he wanted me to know that he had moved on with his life and was only calling to say, *"Goodbye."*

I sat in my living room, numb and dumbfounded for a half an hour. I could feel the Holy Spirit squeezing the hurt in me. I felt like someone tore my heart out of my body and left me to die. I called Ms. Jackie and told her what happened. She told me to come over. I went to her house and wept until my eyes hurt. She comforted and counseled me in her usual way. I was traumatized and confused, but through it all I still loved Jesus. Time heals all wounds and after two months, he was a married man. All I could say was, *"To God be the Glory!"* I love the Lord and nothing can separate me from His love –

neither height, nor depth, nor any other creature, shall be able to separate us from the love of God, which is in Christ Jesus our Lord.

~Romans 8:39~

Today we still talk as if nothing happened. I was proof to everyone that God can give you a heart of forgiveness like no other. I respect his wife and his family because through all of that, I now possess a heart of forgiveness. Forgiveness is powerful and I believe if he was mine, then he would have been with me. No need to carry old baggage despite the hurt it causes. God's grace and mercy will always suffice and carry us through anything life gives us.

And above all things have fervent charity among yourselves: for charity shall cover the multitude of sins. ~1 Peter 4:8~

Chapter Thirteen
Sifting

*And the Lord said, Simon, Simon, behold, Satan hath desired to have **you**, that he may **sift you** as wheat. ~Luke 22:31~*

Many times people are envious when they see others prospering, not understanding the process they had to go through to get where they are. I had to live with things I never imagined would happen to me and the journey was just beginning.

I was struggling and couldn't find any answers, until one day I got a call from a friend. At first, we were talking and laughing, and then he told me about a man who admired me and my ministry. He explained that this man had seen me sing several times. I had a secret admirer and didn't know it. However, considering all that I had experienced over the past months, I wasn't interested in meeting anyone. He proceeded to tell me that the man was previously married. After his wife cheated and left him, they were divorced. He knew I would be angry because I didn't believe in divorce. I got upset with my friend. I hurried him off the phone and plead the blood of Jesus so loudly, you could hear me from a mile away.

After a few days, my friend called me back. He knew that I needed a job and thought it would be a good idea for me to call the secret admirer, because he was a business man. I was really desperate - I owed rent, the light and water bills. My landlord was living in England at the time and although he was very patient with me, something had to be done before his patience ran out. So, I called my secret admirer; his name was Will.

I introduced myself and let him know that, like Ruth - I was only looking for a job, nothing else. He began to tell me things any woman would want to hear. He said that he admired my ministry very much and that instead of working a secular job, I should concentrate on my ministry. Tell me which woman would not want to hear that? I believed he was right, but I insisted on getting a job. I explained that my rent and other bills were almost three - months past due. Nevertheless, he was adamant that I should not work.

We spoke on the phone regularly and became friends. One day he invited me out, and I was curious to meet him in person. He gave me some money to help with my situation, but I made it clear that I was only interested in friendship. After that, strange things started happening. I was having these encounters where I felt like I was not a part of this world. For days I felt like I was captured and held in a cage. I did not talk to him again for about six months.

I relocated to Kingston and was living with a man of God named, Elder Beersingh and his wife, Cutie. They were a really caring couple who treated me as a daughter. They loved God and would always sit and listen to what I had to say. For a while I worked in a clothing store, but the owner and I had a clash of personalities. I think there was something she just didn't like about me. So, I decided to quit working and focus on my true passion - singing.

Before I left Clarendon I was working on a project with a producer named Hugh Campbell. Although he was not a Christian, Hugh liked my voice and decided to produce my album. He saw something in me that no one else saw. He encouraged me to pursue my passion and thought it was time for the world to experience my music. I wrote a song called *Jesus is Alive*; it became an instant hit in Jamaica. From there, we did an album with the same title. The project was finished and released to the public. Although I was becoming known in Jamaica, something was wrong - I was not the same Judith. The Beersingh's had taken me in as their daughter, but one day an argument arose and I got angry. Right there and then I turned from them, not realizing that the enemy was at work.

We never know the path our lives will take and we can't be too anointed for the enemy to want a piece of us. Job was not looking for trouble, but Satan was going to and fro on earth seeking whomever he could devour. He saw the hedge around Job and had the courage to ask God to remove it. God granted his request and gave Job to the devil. He took his children and his cattle and inflicted him with sores, but he could not touch his life. At that time I didn't understand that we can't blame the devil for everything. There are times when God will put us in the heat of the fire to prove our trustworthiness and His powerfulness. Our fiery trials come to make us strong (1 Peter 4:12). When Jesus rose from the dead, we were given full access to the power of God. Let us stop going around like chickens without heads - we are more than conquerors through Christ. Many of us will face things that will seem strange to us, but it is not strange to God. Whatever winds blow in your life, do not try to calm them - just let go and let God.

Chapter Fourteen
Brokenness

I received a wedding proposal from Will and an invitation to attend his church. Like suction, I was sucked into everything he said. No one could give me advice regarding him; I was led by something I couldn't explain. The day I visited his church, the sermon was taken from

~Luke 22:31~

Peter, Satan has desired to sift you like wheat.

I was confused and gripped with fear, but decided to remain calm. We spent the day together and then returned to Sunday evening service. During service, the Pastor called out three people - I was one of them. He said God told him to pray for us specifically, because we were all Psalmists. After the Pastor spoke, a member from the church also gave me a word. He said, *"God said to tell you that anything you choose to do He is with you."* I received the word and was just happy to know that God spoke.

When Will took me home the following day, I accepted his proposal. He said I made him the happiest man in the world, and he would do everything to make me happy. He started crying and I consoled him as his loving, future wife. One night I had a dream that Will gave me a fruit. After eating the fruit, he turned to me and said there was something in my hair. I took a nearby hose and started washing my hair. Then my hair began falling out; I was almost bald. At the conclusion of the dream, I ran to Ms. Jackie and showed her my hair and she told me to pray. When I woke up the next day I called the Pastor. I told him about the proposal and the dream. He told me it wasn't a good dream, but he didn't think it had anything to do with us, because God already spoke to him and told him we were getting married soon. In my spirit I wasn't comfortable - but the Pastor and other leaders said they were speaking for God, so I listened.

I was now living closer to Will in Mandeville. Elder Beersingh and his wife told me to wait, but others were telling me that God had sent him to take me out of my situation. I was convinced they were right, so we got married on March 9, 2003.

That day was a disaster. I was outside sitting in the car, waiting to be escorted down the aisle. I couldn't figure out what was taking so long. I found out later that the Pastor was waiting for the divorce papers from Will's ex-wife, who was asking if I was a nice person and complaining about him. By law it was necessary to see proof of the divorce and the officiating minister was adamant about not doing it without the papers. Despite this, the Pastor of the church convinced him to do it anyway.

When the Pastor was praying the final prayer to confirm the marriage, I had an uncommon experience. It's not always easy to explain spiritual things, but I will try my best. While he was praying, I saw the words of the prayer bouncing like a ball, around the four corners of the building and never ascending. I left the church wondering if anyone else had the same experience. I was not happy and I could see that my mother and sister were not happy either, but no one said anything.

On our way to our honeymoon I was a nervous wreck -I could not contain myself and fear was taunting me. I started singing to soothe my inner man. We reached the hotel and it became more uncomfortable. Every newly-married couple looks forward to enjoying pleasurable moments with each other on that special night, but for us it couldn't happen.

Unfortunately, Will was in a car accident several weeks earlier. That day we went to counseling after which he put me on a taxi to go home. As soon as I reached my house I got a call to inform me that he was in an accident and I rushed to the scene of the accident. A man was dead and Will had to be moved to a security post to avoid looters, and then taken to the hospital in his hometown. He was immediately admitted, because he was urinating blood. As a result, he could not perform on our honeymoon without suffering terrible pain. We spent three days at the hotel and then returned home.

Shortly after, strange things began happening. Before leaving the hotel, I remember putting the marriage certificate in the car, but upon returning home it was nowhere to be found. I asked the pastor to get another copy for me, but something was amiss. I submitted the papers to the tax department and paid for emergency copies. They gave me a return date to come and pick up the new certificate. I felt like I was living in a nightmare. When I returned they could not find any trace of it. I could not figure out what was going on. I was persistent and submitted another form until eventually, I received them. I later found out that Will got rid of the papers. He had paid for no criminal charges to be filled against him from the accident, and also for the documents to be removed from the system. I was living in hell on earth. As his wife, I had no say in anything and could not do anything right in his eyes.

Though I walk in the midst of trouble, thou wilt revive me: thou shalt stretch forth thine hand against the wrath of mine enemies, and thy right hand shall save me.

~ Psalm 138:7~

Chapter Fifteen

Hell on Earth

After about two weeks of marriage, Will left the house. He said he was staying with his family. My friend Shawna and her husband, who were now living in the Cayman Islands, were visiting on vacation and came to see me. I was glad to have some company in the house. When Shawna saw me, she was shocked. I did not look good at all. I was already a slim person, but I had lost even more weight. They spent the night, and then prayed with me before they left.

I continued to have strange experiences in that house. One night while Will was sleeping I heard strange tongues. I jumped from my bed and knelt by the bed side. The tongues brought fear onto the entire house to the point where I was certain something was not right. He started complaining that he could not sleep at the bed front, so I took the front. While there, I saw something walk over my feet and it came between us on the bed. I could no longer reach over and touch him.

The next morning I was in the kitchen when something else happened. No matter how tightly I covered the cooking-oil bottle, the lid kept coming off. It was as if someone was taking if off. I called Will to come and witness it. He saw it for himself and then smiled.

The strange occurrences began to escalate, but I still could not figure them out. I was no longer able to sit beside Will in the house because there was a force that would prevent me. This man was under heavy *"security guards"* and they were not earthly beings. One night I woke up to see his gun on the night table. He was covered up like a dead man, with only one eye left out and it was turned towards me. I was so frightened. Thank God I didn't have a bad heart.

The following day I called a church sister named Christine and told her about the experience. Christine told me that Will had been complaining of hallucinations. He said that when he looked at me, he saw something else; that's why the gun was there. She told me to be careful.

When I would visit his place of business, it was another drama. I would feel as if a thousand eyes were watching me when I moved. When he consumed any food that I cooked, he would vomit. I could not understand this because my food was cooked with worship. We had a helper in the house that also experienced these weird occurrences. In the evenings we would hear the gate open and the vehicle drive in, but no one would walk through the door. When we looked outside, we didn't see anyone. He would walk in a few minutes later. This continued to happen for a while. The only explanation I could think of was that we lived in a haunted house. I was not happy. As I am writing this section, I am angry against evil doers. May God's judgment take them out for professing to be Christians, but are not. They make the shed blood of Jesus of none effect by choosing mediums over the power of His resurrection. May the wrath of God be their portion and may their hell be hotter than the heat Shadrach, Meshach and Abednego faced in the fiery furnace. Woe to them who take the precious blood of God's Son and making it appear useless.

*Upon the **wicked** he shall rain snares, fire and brimstone, and an horrible tempest: this shall be the portion of their cup.*

~Psalm 11:6~

God's grace and mercy kept me while I was there. Will knew that he was not right from the beginning, and that's why he wanted an anointed vessel – because

"the unbelieving husband is sanctified by the wife."

~1Corinthians 7:14~

He wanted to get rich fast and he did whatever it took. The first time I was sexually intimate with him I had to go to the gynecologist. This is not easy for me to say, but what I was experiencing was awful. The doctor ran tests and the results indicated that I had contracted bacteria that was not meant to be anywhere near the female anatomy. A first, I didn't understand what she meant, so she hesitated, and then proceeded to ask me some personal questions.

I told her that I had heard some contrary rumor about Will's sexuality, but didn't know if they were true. When I had asked him about it, of course he denied the claims. He displayed peculiar and unpleasant behaviors that I didn't really understand. For instance, after using the bathroom he didn't wipe like normal people - instead he would wash himself over the bath tub. One night, I went downstairs and caught him with another man. I couldn't even think straight. In shock, I quickly ran back upstairs. I will just leave that there.

After a while, he stopped going to church. He started disrespecting Jesus and the things of God, and became verbally-abusive towards me. I talked to the pastor about his behavior, but that only made him upset. He complained that I was taking his business out of our home. I could not take it anymore, so I called one of his sisters who lived in England, as she was the only one he would listen to. In our conversation she admitted that God had been dealing with her and her husband concerning Will, and that God revealed that he was in a back-slidden state. After our talk she called him, but how I wish she hadn't because all hell broke loose.

But the LORD is with me as a mighty terrible one: therefore my persecutors shall stumble, and they shall not prevail: they shall be greatly ashamed; for they shall not prosper: their everlasting confusion shall never be forgotten. ~Jeremiah 20:11~

Chapter Sixteen
Terror Strikes

Will came home as usual, but on this particular evening I could definitely tell something was wrong. He came in whistling, but he was very angry. He asked me what I had said to his sister. I tried to make it look good, but it wasn't working. He turned to me and asked me to leave. I held on to him to see if I could make things work. I really just wanted to talk, but there was no sense in trying. He picked me up and threw me down on the ground so hard, that I couldn't even move one of my legs. I crawled out of the room, picked up the phone and called for help. I called Christine and she immediately came to my rescue like an angel on assignment. For as long as I remain on this earth, I will never forget this lady.

Christine brought me to the doctor's office. My leg was in bad shape and I was in a lot of pain. After a thorough examination and x-ray by the doctor, the doctor said my leg didn't look good and that I may not have use of it for a long time. She went on to say that it was the worst sprained ankle she had ever seen. The doctors wanted me to press charges because this was abuse. Christine looked at me and said, *"No, Judith. Don't do it."* The doctor gave her final instructions, and then we left. I was now a one-legged person, dependent on others for everything.

Christine took me home and asked Will to help bring me up the stairs. He refused, saying that I should get up the same way I got down. He then got into his vehicle and left. He left me in the room and gave strict orders to the helper concerning me. He told her that if she fed me or helped me do anything in the house, he would fire her. I cried because I saw that the enemy wanted me dead and only God could help me now. When Will left for work, the helper - Ms. Mack, would assist me to the shower and back to the room. She would also sneak enough food for me to eat and make sure I was comfortable. It was the worst time of my life.

Nights turned into days and the house became a camp for demons. You could literally hear demons trying to tear off the roof at nights. I could barely sleep at night because I was constantly terrorized. One night I heard the door handle turning, but he couldn't get in because I had locked it. Earlier that day I received a call saying I should bolt the door because Will wanted to sacrifice me. I was so glad I locked it. After he couldn't get in through the door, he went to the nearest bedroom window and fired his gun. Fear nearly killed me; I became completely paralyzed.

That same night I talked to Mr. Beersingh on the phone. He asked me if I wasn't afraid to stay in the house. I said no, because I realized that death was staring me in the face. Mr. Beersingh asked me for the pastor's phone number and he called the pastor and told him to get me out of that house, because Will was a mad man.

Christine came the next day and escorted me out of the house while Will was gone. I stayed at the pastor's house for a while, but he then suggested that I go back home. Let me say this to you readers: Demons are real and they need a host to carry them around. Not everything we hear shouting and speaking in tongues is born of God. There are those who are sent out on an assignment to kill God's heritage and they will stop at nothing to fulfill their plan. I will also take this opportunity and address leaders by saying that it is a great privilege that God has called us to lead His people.

Through my journey as a believer I have observed many leaders. Some are crafty and wicked. They compromise with folks because they have money, or because they can prophesy and operate in the gifts. Leaders need to remember that God is the one who gives the gift and that the gift doesn't repent, but man does (Romans 11:29). Some will put you out because you don't have the charisma like these demons, who walk around camouflaging themselves as sheep, when they are really wolves (Matthew 7:15). Let the gift of discernment take control; stop destroying God's heritage for demons, or hell will be the portion of all who do these things.

God revealed this to me one day: *Demons also work by networking. When a chief demon sends out a demon to terrorize God's people and fails, a network is put in place to send other demons to help accomplish the plan. They will continue to send demons out until they are either successful or frustrated. If frustration takes place, it means the believer is in tune with God. It is at that time of frustration that the chief demon will turn up, but the believer doesn't need to worry, because the chief of the believers, JESUS CHRIST, will step in.* The path of our life will be determined by God, but one thing is for sure, after He has tried us, we will come forth as pure gold.

Chapter Seventeen
Back in Hell

I was on a journey, but to where I could not tell you, only God knew. One thing I've realized is that the greater the anointing on a person's life, the greater the challenges they will face. Depression became my middle name and those demons were enjoying it. After I was sent back home, I became a laughing stock and a mockery. Will never ceased to bring women in to make sure they laughed at me. *Why was I ever born and why should I be facing these things?* I used to wonder. I was just an innocent young lady who wanted to live for God and have a good life in the process. This could not be the reason my mother endured the shame of her pregnancy and the difficulty of my birth. Sometimes I wonder why bad things happen to good people, while evil doers live like they own the universe, but God still rules and reigns and I had no choice but to continue to trust Him. Job said it right:

Though he slay me, yet will I trust in him: but I will maintain mine own ways before him. ~Job 13:15~

There are two types of sorrow in this world: Godly sorrow and the sorrow we cause on ourselves. Please make sure you are innocent of every situation occurring in your life that is evil and that you did not willingly get involved with them presumptuously. God will make a way of escape for all situations, but not every believer takes the way.

The Bishop of that organization heard about the situation and decided to come and take me out. Will was not around when he came, but he had told Ms. Mack to take out every piece of clothing that he had bought and to make sure I only had the ones I came with. I walked away from everything, including my hat-making business because it was a part of his two businesses. She complied, and after two and a half months, I left with only those physical things I had brought into the marriage. In addition to this however, I now carried the extra weight of abuse, oppression and depression.

I was taken back to Kingston and was determined to win this war over my soul. When the Bishop came for me I told him that I do not trust anyone who is called pastor, prophet or Bishop. I was becoming a hater of these people because of everything I had seen and endured. From the day I stepped into church I was told lies and sucked financially dry by the strategies these leaders used to collect money. I was getting angry at this man, but he dealt with the situation very well. He was the most humble man I had ever seen.

He placed me in a home with some of the church sisters. Things were good for a while, but the torment was far from being over. One Thursday night I went to Bible study where they were teaching about cults. Through the teaching of the man of God, I realized that was the situation I was in. I had experienced everything that he taught and now that my eyes were open, it would only get worse. When we don't know something, it will not harm us, but once our eyes are opened to the demonic realm, the demons will make sure our life is shortened. This is because they don't want us to tell their secrets.

Soon, the church sisters were being used against me. They complained about any and everything they could find, even that I prayed too loud. Life for me was really bad, but I had to stay with them until I could walk again. My journey to walk again was both long and short. It was long because the doctors told me to keep my leg up and short because out of nowhere, Will called to ask how I was doing. I would hear voices telling me to kill myself. I described how bad my leg was and told him I could not walk. He said, *"Oh my God, you won't walk for now."* I hung up the phone so fast and forgot the doctor's order. I got mad and began shouting that no demon will prophesy over my leg. That same day, one of the pastors from the church in Kingston brought me a pair of crutches, but I told him that I didn't want them. God gave me two legs and I was going to walk on them. I then started hopping around on my leg. The devil was trying to set me up to stay paralyzed, but I refused to stay where the enemy wanted me. Although the doctor's report said I would not walk for a long time, I was walking around after only one month.

> *He disappointeth the **devices** of the crafty, so that their hands cannot perform their enterprise*
>
> ~Job 5:12~

The enemy does not respect persons; he will use anyone who is available and at times, the individual isn't even aware. Life seemed like it was going downhill. No one wanted to stay around me because of the curse I was under, but I was willing to trust God. Although I felt like He was not around me, I knew He was right there. Hebrews 13:5 reminds us that *He will never leave or forsake us*. I started getting sick and kept losing weight. I had no joy and there was no beauty in me. Here is a picture of me at that time.

In spite of everything, I was determined to stand firmly upon God's word and continue to trust Him, because He always sends help. The Bishop decided that it was time for me to move from where I was staying, to another church member's house. This old lady was no ordinary old lady. She would criticize the Bishop and tell me stories about how she had lent him money to purchase a church building and how she had to mortgage her house. That lady could talk!

Being there with her was no joke; the demonic attacks I was having were not meant for humans to handle. I was seeing things beyond this world. I heard voices telling me to kill myself because there was no hope for me. When I would kneel to pray, they were demanding me to stop. Those spirits were waging war against me. One night I got up and went to the bathroom. Upon returning to bed, I heard voices talking at the back door and the sound of drums beating. I held my head, thinking it was the obeah man from the community, but it would not stop. This occurred on three occasions, but only when I lay down to sleep.

The voices became more intense, so I sat up in the bed. I felt like my feet were on fire and that my breath was being sucked from my body. I held on to my throat and felt something pick me up from the bed and threw me in the air. I landed on my feet and entered into warfare. That was one scary night, but by His grace I was able to overcome.

The talkative, little old lady started reporting me to the pastor. She complained that I played my music and prayed loudly. Her rules were very strict and I tried to obey them as much as I could; I would even have to make sure her utensils were a certain way on the dinner plate. One day the pastor of the church called me and asked to have a meeting with the elders about *"grandma's"* complaint. She sat there gloating as I tried to defend myself, but to no avail. Though I was innocent of the things I was accused of doing, I was rebuked in front of everyone, but I took it and went home.

When we arrived home, the lady told me she was caught off guard and that I wasn't doing anything like what she told the pastor. I told her to call and tell them the truth, but she said, *"No, let it stay"*. I could not believe my ears, and I was wounded. I called another pastor for advice and he told me to leave, because too much was happening to me in that church, but I disregarded his suggestion and remained.

Not long after my first album launch, *The Sun Shines Again*, *"Grandma"* thought I made some money. One evening she came to me and told me God said I should leave her house. She then took her keys and locked the door. I had to walk through the neighbor's house to leave. That same evening I was on my way to a tent crusade in Marverly, in Kingston, Jamaica. I never wavered in my faith. I just went with the intention of giving God praise. I was determined to stay focused and trust God. After the crusade, I did not have anywhere to go so I decided to stay under the tent after everyone was gone, but they were pulling down the tent that night. I had to think fast, because everyone was leaving and I could not be on the street alone. I kept praying to God to intervene and then I remembered I had the number for a church sister. I called her and asked if I could stay with her for the night. She told me to come.

When I arrived at her house and told her the situation, she empathized with me and thought *"Grandma"* was evil for the way she had treated me. One evening she came home and saw me on her phone. She left the house for about twenty minutes and I was still on the phone. It was not idle conversation. Someone was trying to negotiate with me about a concert, but they kept hanging up and calling back until they reached a consensus with their partner. When she saw me on the phone for that length of time, she was furious. She said I was on her phone too long and that I had to leave. She took my things and threw them in the passage and told me to get out of her house. I humbly picked my things up and cried. I did not know the first thing to do, but whatever the cost I was willing to go with Jesus all the way.

The landlord was living in the building so I waited until she arrived. I knew she had an empty room on the property and I was hoping she would let me rent it. I let her know that I couldn't pay the rent right now, but she still said yes and I moved in. Although I had just launched my album, I didn't have any money because I had to pay back the man who loaned me the money to get the CD's from the pressing plant. That alone was a miracle.

Days before the launch, I struggled to get the CD's - but God showed me what to do. I had a dream where I met this man named Basil. He came to me and helped me with some plants that were flourishing at the top, but needed to be watered at the root. Basil took them, watered them and told me he would come back to water the rest. I saw the dream manifest before my eyes.

I was always going to help out churches wherever and whenever I could. One night, The Full Truth Church of God was having a service in one of our remote areas in Jamaica. After the service was over, I was taken away in a trance and started speaking in tongues. I came out of it when my phone started ringing in my pocket. To my surprise, it was Basil asking me what's going on with my CD's. I told him and he decided to loan me the money. He even went a step further and loaned me the money for the rental of the room. Now I understood why he told me (in the dream) that he would come back to water the rest. Paul said he plants, Apollo watered, but it is God who gives the increase (1Corinthians 3:6). God would have it so that my CD's started selling and I would gather enough to reimburse Basil. I pray God's strength for those men, like Basil, who are obedient to the call of God and are willing to do for others according to how God has given them wisdom.

I have never seen the righteous forsaken nor his seed begging bread ~Psalm 37:25~

Chapter Eighteen

He Never Fails

Our future is not planned by us or our parents, but God is the one who designed it all to get His glory. God told Jeremiah that before he was formed He knew him, and

before thou came out of thy mother's womb I sanctified thee and ordained thee a prophet to the nations.

~Jeremiah 1:5~

God knows what will befall every one of us, but He also thinks good thoughts and has a plan (Jeremiah 29:11). None of us are here by mistake and we need to know that.

I stayed at the house for a while. The only thing I had was my clothes, (they were more like rags) but I was determined to stay with Jesus. The demonic forces were unbearable and prevented me from sleeping at nights. I was tired and depressed because I wasn't getting any rest. Will had sent his message that he would not stop until I died, but I kept consecrated before God, knowing He would avenge me one day.

Yea, though I walk through the valley of the shadow of death, I will fear no evil: for thou art with me, thy rod and thy staff they comfort me. Thou preparest a table before me in the presence of mine enemies; thou anointest my head with oil; my cup runneth over. Surely goodness and mercy shall follow me all the days of my life: and I shall dwell in the house of the Lord for ever. ~Psalm 23:4-6~

By this time, I was going to the church during the days to sleep because at nights it was excruciating. One night I was home alone because the other young lady was no longer living in the house. I had an experience that allowed me to know again that God is real. I felt fear coming up on me and I started seeing things I cannot explain. They came for me and this time they were determined. I gained some courage and prayed, *"God give me a song, for You said idols will be destroyed through my singing."* Like a scroll, He gave me a melody and the following words.

Stand still and know that I am God, Stand still and know I'm not too far and I will be with you every step of the way. When you walk through the valley of the shadow of death, I am there with you, when you go through the fire, oh no, the flames will not burn, when death seems to be waiting to take you away, remember your time is not yet, you don't watch the storms you just watch Me. I am the resurrection and the life! My Father has given Me a name that is above every other name, and at My name every knee shall bow and every tongue must confess that I am Lord, that I am Lord! So, stand still and know that I am God.

I felt and saw when everything disappeared. I will never doubt the power of God for as long as I live, and that's what makes the devil mad. When I was growing up in the country, I often heard folks talk about *"duppies"*, but now I realized those things were jokes compared to what I was experiencing. These things were from the pit of hell. I would feel like something was poking me in my eyes and then my eyes would just get swollen. When I stood up, something came and tried to push me down. Through it all, I was determined not to give up on God. I became a lover of God's word.

*Thou art worthy, O Lord, to receive glory and honour and power: for thou hast **created** all things, and for thy pleasure **they** are and **were created**.*

~Revelation 4:11~

Reading this passage reminds me that God is in charge; therefore my confidence is boosted and I know He is able to see me through.

Eventually, God enabled me to leave the house shortly after discovering the owners were into satanic practices and dedicated the house as a place of worship. Without hesitation, I packed what little I had and moved out! Praise be to God! He does work miracles. We never know the avenue God will use to get us out of our situation. My sister, Maria, who was living in Westmoreland, became sick and decided to attend a church service in the parish. There was a pastor visiting from Canada who preached and my sister was convicted. She gave her life to the Lord and decided to give the pastor a gift - it was my CD.

He took the CD back to Canada and gave it to the secretary. She was having a ball with the CD. Oh, how she would boast about the anointing that was upon the CD. Every morning when he got to work, she would tell him that he had to get me there to sing. Finally, he was convinced. One day I got some money from a bank, which I should not have received, so I decided to bring it back to them. While I was there, I got a phone call from a gentleman who introduced himself as Dr. Audley James, from Revival Tabernacle. He said he loved my CD and would love to bring me to the church for their Anniversary.

I believe God set me up that day. Had I not returned that money, I believe my blessing would have been lost. He arranged for me to get the necessary documents for me to travel. In less than a month, I was in Canada. I was only supposed to stay for three days, but with God's intervention - I stayed for three weeks.

My name was spreading like wild fire and everyone wanted to have me in their church. I must salute my father and mentor - a true man of God, Dr. Audley James. He is the man God used to show me favor. Sir, may you be blessed continually in all you do and may your life on this earth be emulated by others.

As I previously mentioned, I had lost everything. One day, I told Dr. James that I will not leave until God gives me the money to either buy a car or instructs someone to bless me with one. I just spoke by faith, knowing that

faith cometh by hearing and by hearing the word of God

~Romans 10:17~

I left a week after speaking that word to the man of God and I can tell you that it came to pass. Yes, I was blessed to go home with more than enough! I was able to buy a car, rent and furnish another apartment and start life over again.

Life was going pretty good, but I still had to deal with the warfare. I was invited back to Canada and the visits were just getting better and better. I became a household name in Canada and I will be forever grateful to those who contributed in the process. I left from there to England with Evangelist Vanessa Anderson. God used that woman to tell me all I was going through and how He would deliver me. She poured into my life and was very instrumental in my spiritual growth. Her favorite quote to me was, *"Walk softly before God"*. I will never forget the warm heart of God's choice servant.

Spiritual warfare was an on-going thing, but God was on my side. One night I was walking up my steps when I felt like singing. Although I'm a singer – I rarely sing for the sake of singing, but that night I could not stop. I went to bed singing and about five minutes into my sleep, I felt like someone threw something in my face. You could not imagine the pain I was experiencing. I got up from the bed and turned on the lights. I looked like someone who had leprosy. This was not normal, but I found myself laughing. I then looked on my dresser and saw a bottle of olive oil. I asked God to transform that oil into His blood. I began praying for God to burn these things off my face with His fire. I told the devil that he crossed the border by touching God's anointed. I warred that night and told the devil they must be gone when I wake in the morning. I got up the next day and they were not there.

No weapon formed against God's people can prosper.

~Isaiah 54:17~

Yes, weapons will form but they can't and will not prosper because Jesus died and rose from the grave, and gave us authority over everything; therefore, I refuse to live my life in defeat to please the enemy. The devil is a liar. I am very passionate about this part; The blood of Jesus prevails every time.

Chapter Nineteen
Victory is Mine

A local church was holding a crusade and the speaker was a pastor from Nigeria. He made an altar call and I went up for prayer. After laying hands on me, I could not stop laughing; God restored my joy. It was a feeling I wish every sad person could experience. The restoration of one's joy is a divinely-orchestrated occurrence that cannot be explained by human wisdom.

Hugh never gave up on me and we were able to finish the second album, *The Sun Shines Again.* God gave a young lady named Kerian Johnson, a revelation to write this song that has restored lives and revived worshippers. She may never fully understand why God allowed her to pen that song for me, but only God can give someone the wisdom to write like that. On the day that song was sent to me, something prophetic happened - the sun was shining and the rain was falling. God restored my soul and if He did it for me, He will do it for you.

I have been through so many things in my life and I can't really talk about everything in this book, but in all the drama and trauma I've been through - I really want to leave this legacy in this chapter. Never doubt that God will avenge you of all the trials; never stop trusting in the power of the blood of Jesus. There are times when the days and nights may seem long and you might become weary. In your weariness hope seems nonexistent, but hope that is seen is not hope (Romans 8:24). You will soon rejoice in dancing and singing again. The price was paid through Jesus' blood. The stage is now set for the show and God will watch you as you give Him praise for the victory you will have.

I opened a business and needed some goods for it. I met a business man who told me he would furnish the store with all the goods I needed and I agreed. After making the deal with the man, I went home feeling real good. I was getting the goods the following day, but I had a dream the night before that I was walking into his store half naked. Before I could enter the store, a lady met me and said, *"You can't go in like that."* She took a white sheet and covered me, then said, *"You can go in now"*. I got up in the morning and asked God for covering before I went to the store.

As I sat there counting the goods, I felt when something fell from above and covered me; I felt a peace that cannot be explained. After that encounter, I experienced an amazing surprise. I saw a man walk in the store, but it was more like an apparition (he wasn't in the building). I could feel that others were physically there, but this particular man could not be identified. It was Will, and he appeared like a man without a soul. I sat still under the covering of God until he left.

After I was finished and took my journey back to my store, I returned to earth with a heavenly mantle upon me. I heard God talking to me while I sat in my office. He said *"that which you experienced today was meant to disgrace you, but I protected you."* I felt when righteous indignation arose in me, and I stretched my hands to the heavens and prayed, *"God may the hand that rise against me and the tongues that speak evil against me never live to tell another tale."* Someone held my hand up in the air and I knew it was God.

That day, I felt empowered and delivered, and I knew something supernatural had happened. I was always having strange dreams about Will and how disaster had struck his house. I would beg God to let me go and tell him to repent. The forces of darkness that this man was entangled with were so powerful, that I could not go back to Mandeville where he lived. I had no doubt that he was still employing demons to attack me. I would drive my brand new car through the town and for no apparent reason, it would break down. Hell was trying to have a show-down on earth. My friends, the experience with those demonic spirits is one I would never wish on my worst enemy. God's mercy kept me, so I didn't give up. I knew God would avenge me for all the lies he told on me and for the slander he built against my name. Furthermore, I knew God would have vindicated me of him, because he was brazen enough to enter into God's sheepfold and attempt to destroy one of His prized possessions. I just didn't know when it would happen; but God is an on-time God. Yes, He is!

One morning after finishing my devotion, I just could not get out of bed. I felt like a house was on top of me. I lay still for a moment, and then I heard the phone ring. It was my sister calling to ask me the name of the man to whom I was married. When I told her, she shockingly informed me that he was dead. Someone had called to tell her, but I could not believe it. I ended the conversation and immediately called the young man who introduced Will and me, and he confirmed that it was true. I still didn't believe him either, so he told me to call the guy that was currently living at the house, and he also confirmed the news.

When the reality finally set in, I started a search in the spirit realm to tell him to repent, but it was effortless. He was repeatedly warned to leave his evil lifestyle and take back his position in God, but he preferred the money. Rather than having a Savior who could give him all he needed, he sold his soul for money and loved it.

Days later, I spoke to his beloved sister who came from England. She told me about the things she had found in the house and it was heart-wrenching. He was

115

deep into the occult and had been ordained as a priest. I found out that he really wanted to sacrifice me as well. They found letters where he wrote things about me and their plans for me. She told me she burned them all. On top of that, his male lovers started coming around her and she became angry.

Although I didn't go to his funeral, his sister told me about the procession. She walked out of the funeral service because the pastor was giving the wicked dead man underserved praised. She wanted to scream at them, because she knew her brother died a reprobate.

After Will's funeral, I received multiple apologies from pastors and church members alike. No one wanted to believe me when I told the truth about his wrong doings because he had money; but God has a way of showing everyone how mighty and strong He is. God delivered me and I owe my life to Him. Truly, He has caused me to triumph over my enemies (2 Corinthians 2:14).

While I can advise anyone who reads this book to be careful, I can also say that you can never be too careful for the enemy to choose you as a target. I would have rather seen his soul restored before his departure from this life, but God has given all of us a choice - to choose good over evil- and Will made his choice. Scripture tells about what the love of money will do, but so many people still continue to build their lives on the foundation of earthly things and on not things above. You may not like the results, but you will reap what you sow.

Be encouraged everyone, I am still in God's hands and going through my processing, which will continue until Jesus returns. Indeed, the journey continues.

Though I walk in the midst of trouble, thou wilt revive me: thou shalt stretch forth thine hand against the wrath of mine enemies, and thy right hand shall save me.

~Psalm 138:7~

Chapter Twenty
Lessons Learnt

Every spiritual storm that we have to pass through in life should be dealt with just the same as natural storms. In a natural storm, there is always debris to get rid of. In like manner, we should also lose some things in the spiritual storm, namely the works of the flesh.

~James 5:19-21~

Now the works of the flesh are manifest, which are these; Adultery, fornication, uncleanness, lasciviousness, [20] *Idolatry, witchcraft, hatred, variance, emulations, wrath, strife, seditions, heresies,* [21] *Envying, murders, drunkenness, reveling.*

As we strive to rid our lives of those things, we must gain something out of it. Galatians 5:22-23 should be what we get out.

~Galatians 5:22-23~

But the fruit of the Spirit is love, joy, peace, longsuffering, gentleness, goodness, faith, 23 Meekness, temperance: against such there is no law.

These life lessons must be learned and after words we ought to be ready and willing to teach others how to overcome. Jesus said, *"Peter the devil is out to sift you like wheat"* (Luke 22:31) Jesus would have allowed Peter to know that there was a storm coming, and so with that Peter would have to learn a few lessons, but he guaranteed the victory because Jesus prayed for him. Jesus did the same for us; He said

"Father do not take them out of this world but keep them in it".

~John 17:15~

Jesus knew that everyone of us would go through challenging moments, or spiritual storms, but because He already went through them, He made the yoke easier and lighter. Therefore, the challenges we now experience are the vibration of what was already conquered, and our victory is already sealed. I am now living a victorious life. Like a uniformed officer wearing a bullet proof vest, when hit by the bullet, that officer is fully protected if he is not hit in uncovered places. He will feel the impact of the bullet, but is not wounded beyond repair. We as the believers should always wear our full armor so that we can withstand against the wiles of the devil (Ephesian 6:11) when the enemy comes he is coming in for a kill and not to befriend with us. Never the less do not fear. Our storms are designed to take us to our destiny. Though they come with heavy winds and rain, the rain is good for watering and the wind will propel you to your destiny. I learn in the storms of life to adopt the character of the palm tree, though the ferocious wind blow the branches off, causing it to bend a little, it has such deep root in the ground that it will grow back stronger than before, I want to describe that as being anchored in Jesus. Blow storm, blow, but I will be raised up after you are gone, because no storm lasts forever; they come only to do a job. I was Broken to be Blessed and I am Destined to Win, and I've learned to endure hardship like a good soldier (2 Timothy 2:3) I have also learned to trust God and obey His word. Walk softly before Him, depend on Him, bind, rebuke, forgive, and most of all, love even when it seems impossible.

Contact Information

Judith Gayle Ministries International

Website: www.judithgayle.net
Email: jgaylew@gmail.com
Jamaica & Caribbean:
1(876) 441-4422
Canada (416) 625-2526
United States (904) 352-7369

Available CDs & Book by Judith Gayle

 I Believe

 Designed to Worship

 Broken to Be Blessed

 The Sun Shines Again

Preserving The Soul

Orville Campbell

RN, RM, BSCN, MSCN & ED

917 346 6274